S0-BRW-610

CARMEL CLAY PUBLIC LIBRARY

ILLINOIS

Rennay Craats

www.av2books.com

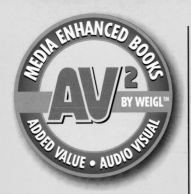

AV² provides enriched content that supplements and complements this book. Weigl's AV² books strive to create inspired learning and engage young minds in a total learning experience.

Your AV² Media Enhanced books come alive with...

Audio
Listen to sections of the book read aloud.

Key Words
Study vocabulary, and complete a matching word activity.

Video
Watch informative video clips.

Quizzes
Test your knowledge.

Embedded Weblinks
Gain additional information for research.

Slide Show
View images and captions, and prepare a presentation.

Try This!
Complete activities and hands-on experiments.

... and much, much more!

Go to **www.av2books.com**, and enter this book's unique code.

BOOK CODE

K 6 4 5 7 7 9

AV² by Weigl brings you media enhanced books that support active learning.

Published by AV² by Weigl
350 5th Avenue, 59th Floor
New York, NY 10118
Website: www.av2books.com

Copyright © 2017 AV² by Weigl
All rights reserved. No part of this publication may be reproduced, stored in a retrieval system, or transmitted in any form or by any means, electronic, mechanical, photocopying, recording, or otherwise, without the prior written permission of the publisher.

Library of Congress Cataloging-in-Publication Data
Names: Craats, Rennay, author.
Title: Illinois : the Prairie State / Rennay Craats.
Description: New York, NY : AV2 by Weigl, 2016. | Series: Discover America |
  Includes index.
Identifiers: LCCN 2015048009 (print) | LCCN 2015049092 (ebook) | ISBN
  9781489648549 (hard cover : alk. paper) | ISBN 9781489648556 (soft cover :
  alk. paper) | ISBN 9781489648563 (Multi-User eBook)
Subjects: LCSH: Illinois--Juvenile literature.
Classification: LCC F541.3 C732 2016 (print) | LCC F541.3 (ebook) | DDC 977.3--dc23
LC record available at http://lccn.loc.gov/2015048009

Printed in the United States of America, in Brainerd, Minnesota
1 2 3 4 5 6 7 8 9   20 19 18 17 16

042016
040816

Project Coordinator Heather Kissock
Art Director Terry Paulhus

Photo Credits
Every reasonable effort has been made to trace ownership and to obtain permission to reprint copyright material. The publisher would be pleased to have any errors or omissions brought to their attention so that they may be corrected in subsequent printings. The publisher acknowledges Getty Images, Corbis Images, iStock, Wikimedia, and Alamy as its primary image suppliers for this title.

ILLINOIS

Contents

AV² Book Code 2
Discover Illinois 4

THE LAND
Beginnings 6
Where is Illinois? 8
Land Features 10
Climate 12
Nature's Resources 14
Vegetation 16
Wildlife 18

ECONOMY
Tourism 20
Primary Industries 22
Goods and Services 24

HISTORY
Native Americans 26
Exploring the Land 28
The First Settlers 30
History Makers 32

CULTURE
The People Today 34
State Government 36
Celebrating Culture 38
Arts and Entertainment 40
Sports and Recreation 42

Get to Know Illinois 44
Brain Teasers 46
Key Words/Index 47
Log on to www.av2books.com 48

STATE ANIMAL
White-tailed Deer

STATE BIRD
Cardinal

STATE FLAG
Illinois

ILLINOIS

STATE FLOWER
Violet

STATE TREE
White Oak

STATE SEAL
Illinois

Nickname
The Prairie State

Motto
State Sovereignty,
National Union

Song
"Illinois," words by Charles
H. Chamberlain and music by
Archibald Johnston

Population
(2010 Census) 12,830,632
Ranked 5th state

Entered the Union
December 3, 1818, as the 21st state

Capital
Springfield

Discover Illinois

Near the center of the United States lies Illinois, a state renowned for its farms and factories as well as the city of Chicago. Located in the northeast corner of the state, Chicago is the third-largest city in the country and a national leader in finance and technology. Walking along its busy streets, it is difficult to imagine the prairies that covered the land just a few hundred years ago. Back then, prairies stretched as far as the eye could see, earning Illinois its official nickname, the Prairie State. Illinois is often also referred to as the Land of Lincoln, which is the state slogan.

Although the state may be known for its prairie, that is not the only type of terrain in Illinois. Forests, cliffs, and lakes can all be found in the state. Illinois has 73 state parks and 12 state recreation areas. Visitors can take advantage of the outdoors and experience the state's natural landscape by biking, cross country skiing, hiking, and boating.

Chicago is one of the most diverse places in the nation. People from more than 100 ethnic groups call the city home and bring to Illinois a wide range of customs, traditional foods, and cultural interests, notably in music. Chicago's various annual music festivals bring energy and excitement to the city.

The Land

The Herald Square Monument is a bronze statue in downtown Chicago featuring George Washington, Robert Morris, and Haym Solomon.

Illinois has 102 counties.

Almost 10,000 miles of train tracks run through the state.

Chicago was settled at the mouth of the Chicago River, where the Mississippi River and Lake Michigan connect.

Beginnings

The early pioneers who settled in Illinois built a successful farm-based economy. While agriculture remains important in the state, Illinois is now home to a wide range of industries. From commerce and trade to digital technology and health care, Illinois is forging ahead with the pioneer spirit of its founders.

The French were the first settlers to the Illinois area. They controlled the Mississippi River Valley from the late 1600s to the mid 1700s. In 1778, U.S. militia men from Virginia won control of the area.

When Illinois entered the union in 1818, the state had 34,620 residents. Due to the fertile farm lands, **immigrants** from England, Germany, and the eastern parts of the U.S. began putting down roots in the state. When industry and mining began in the early to mid-1800s, the settlers had an even greater economic reason to stay.

In 1851, 2.5 million acres of Illinois land were used for the Illinois Central Railroad. Farmers prospered with the railroad because the goods grown on farms could be shipped all over the state. The land became more valuable, bringing more people and more business to Illinois.

Where is
ILLINOIS?

Three rivers and five states border Illinois. The Mississippi River separates Illinois from Iowa and Missouri to the west. The Ohio River separates southeastern Illinois from Kentucky. The Wabash River forms part of the state's border with Indiana, which lies to the east. The far northeastern part of Illinois is bordered by part of Lake Michigan. Wisconsin forms the northern border.

IOWA

MISSOURI

KANSAS

United States Map

Alaska   Hawai'i

→ Illinois

MAP LEGEND

- ■ Illinois
- ☆ Capital City
- ● Major City
- ▲ Mormon Pioneer Trail
- ⬗ Trail of Tears State Forest
- ☐ Bordering States
- ☐ Water

SCALE

0   50 miles

---

1 Springfield

Springfield is the capital of Illinois. The city became the capital of the state in 1839. During the Civil War, Springfield was a training center for Grant's army. Businesses and railroads were built to support the war effort and encouraged a population boom for the area.

2 Peoria

One of the oldest settlements in the state, Peoria was established as a trading and shipping center. The city was named after the Peoria Native Americans. Today, visitors can attend plays at the Peoria Players Theatre, see the Peoria Symphony Orchestra, or visit one of the city's many museums.

WISCONSIN

Lake Michigan

MICHIGAN

ILLINOIS

2 → ○**Peoria**

▲

3 ↑

☆ **Springfield**

1 ↑

INDIANA

4 ↓

KENTUCKY

---

3 **Mormon Pioneer Trail**

The Mormon Pioneer Trail spans five states. It marks the journey that more than 70,000 Mormons took from the 1840s–1860s while seeking religious freedom. The trail begins in Nauvoo, Illinois, and ends in Salt Lake City, Utah. Visitors can drive the trail and stop at key locations along the way.

4 **Trail of Tears State Forest**

At slightly more than 5,000 acres, the Trail of Tears State Forest pays tribute to the Native Americans who were forced from their homes by European settlers. Today, visitors can camp, hunt, and hike on the grounds. The Union State Nursery occupies 120 acres of the park and produces 3 million seedlings per year.

Land Features

Illinois has four major land regions. They are the Central Lowland, the Ozark Plateaus, the Interior Low Plateaus, and the Coastal Plain. The Central Lowland, created during the last Ice Age by **glaciers**, covers about 90 percent of the state. The Ozark Plateaus, the second major land region, are found along the Mississippi River in the southwest. The Interior Low Plateaus, or Shawnee Hills, sprawl across the southern part of Illinois. The Coastal Plain at the southern tip of Illinois is hilly toward the north and flat in the south.

Illinois has as many as 900 rivers and streams. Most of them flow into the mighty Mississippi River, on the state's western border. Illinois's rivers, streams, and lakes provide drinking water for the state's citizens, as well as a means of transportation.

Ozark Plateaus

Horseshoe Lake is located in a low flood plain that follows the Mississippi River down to the state's border with Kentucky.

Central Lowland

The Central Lowland contains such geographic features as shallow river valleys and fertile plains.

Interior Low Plateaus

The Interior Low Plateaus contain the Shawnee Hills, which are covered with forestland.

Coastal Plain

Illinois's Coastal Plain region is generally flat, with very productive land.

Climate

Illinois has cold, snowy winters and hot, wet summers. The southern part of the state is typically warmer than the north. Illinois gets an average of about 39 inches of precipitation each year. Severe thunderstorms and deadly tornadoes can occur.

In summer, the state's average temperature is about 75°F. Winter temperatures average about 30°F, although they can plunge below freezing for weeks at a time. The hottest recorded temperature was 117°F, on July 14, 1954, in East St. Louis. The coldest was –36° F, on January 5, 1999, in Congerville.

Average Annual Precipitation Across Illinois

The average annual precipitation varies for different areas across Illinois. How does location affect the amount of precipitation an area receives?

LEGEND
Average Annual Precipitation (in inches) 1961–1990

200 – 100.1

100 – 25.1

25 – 5 and less

IOWA

Mississippi

MISSOURI

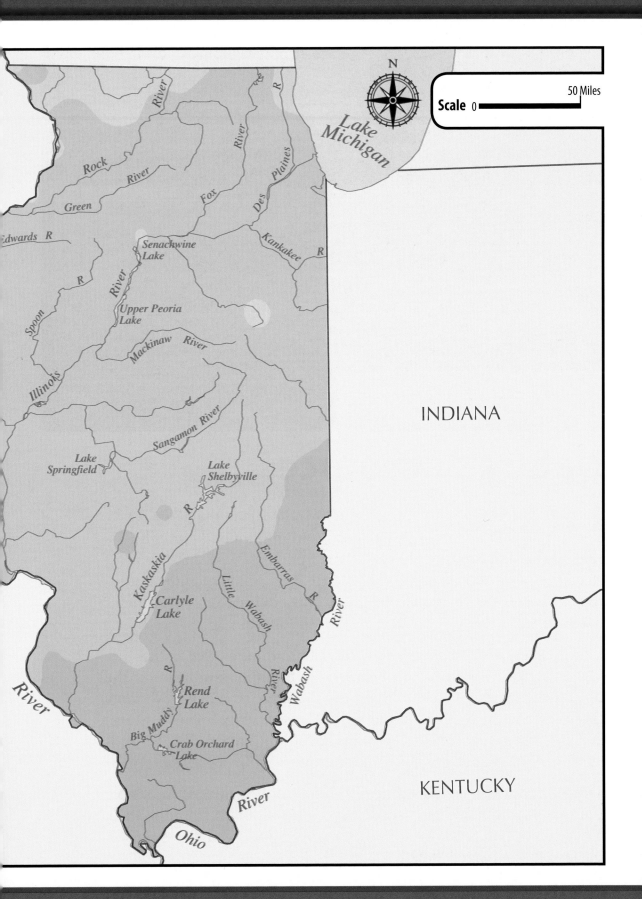

Lake
Michigan

N

Rock

River

River

Green

Fox

Des
Plaines

Edwards R

Senachwine
Lake

Kankakee R

R

River

Spoon

Upper Peoria
Lake

Mackinaw River

Illinois

Sangamon River

Lake
Springfield

Lake
Shelbyville

R

INDIANA

Kaskaskia

Embarras

R

River

Carlyle
Lake

Little

Wabash

Wabash

River

R

Rend
Lake

Big Muddy

Crab Orchard
Lake

River

KENTUCKY

River

Ohio

Illinois is ranked second in the U.S. in coal production, with more than 60 million tons of coal mined each year. Coal brings $1.5 billion to the state economy annually.

Nature's Resources

Illinois is rich in natural resources. Oil and coal are the two most commercially important resources found in Illinois. Although **reserves** are large, oil supplies less than 1 percent of the state's electrical power. Nuclear power and coal-fired plants provide more than 90 percent of the state's electricity. Most of the rest comes from natural gas.

Illinois is one of the leading producers of bituminous coal in the United States. This type of coal is found in basinlike landforms in the central and southern parts of the state. Demand for coal is lower now than it was in the first half of the 1900s. This is partly because when coal is burned, it produces a great deal of sulfur, carbon dioxide, and other gases that contribute to air pollution.

Tripoli, a rock that contains tiny bits of quartz, is produced in Illinois. Industrial sand, used in glass-making, is also exported from the state. The town of Galena, in western Illinois, once produced 85 percent of the lead in the United States.

Illinois is ranked 26th in the United States in natural gas production. In the production of crude oil, Illinois is ranked 15th.

Tripoli is used in ceramics, polishing, and in paint.

With six nuclear power stations, Illinois generates the most nuclear energy than any other state in the U.S.

Vegetation

Before the early settlers arrived, most of what is now northern and central Illinois was covered with tall-grass prairie, and southern Illinois was thick with woodlands. Although much of the land has been cleared for agriculture and industry, the state retains many beautiful natural areas. Today, woodlands and forests cover about 6,400 square miles of Illinois. The state's forests are filled mostly with hardwood trees such as black walnut, maple, and oak. Other common trees include sycamore, mulberry, black cherry, ash, pine, dogwood, and hackberry.

The state's official flower is the violet. This delicate purple flower is found all over Illinois, most commonly in meadows and forests. Many other wildflowers are found in the state. Tall, graceful black-eyed Susans flourish along roadsides, buttercups spread across the grasses, and goldenrod and bluebells bloom almost everywhere.

Black-Eyed Susans

Black-eyed Susans are found in all counties of Illinois. They can grow to more than 2 feet tall.

Prairie Blazing Stars

This common wildflower, which is said to resemble a fairy's wand, is often found in prairies and meadows. It can grow up to 5 feet tall.

Black Walnut Tree

Black walnut trees are among the many types of hardwood trees found in the state.

Violets

There are hundreds of types of violets found around the world. While purple is the most common color, violets can also be blue, yellow, or white.

Wildlife

Various mammal **species** can be found in Illinois. Muskrats, minks, and beavers are found near rivers and lakes. Woodchucks, opossums, skunks, deer, foxes, and coyotes inhabit wooded areas. Squirrels and raccoons are common both in the forests and in urban and suburban areas.

Birdlife in Illinois is exceptionally diverse, from the common robins and pigeons to the elusive red-tailed hawks and Eastern screech owls. Some species, such as the purple finch and redheaded woodpecker, are permanent residents. Others, such as the turkey vulture and indigo bunting, are seasonal visitors.

Water pollution has almost wiped out many species of fish in Illinois. Despite this, there are lots of bass, carp, catfish, and bullheads remaining. Sportfishing is popular in the state.

Red Fox

Red foxes can be found in urban areas as well as around forests, in grasslands, and in agricultural regions. They can run up to 30 miles per hour.

Bluegill

The bluegill was adopted as the state fish in 1986. A member of the sunfish family, it is found throughout the state, mostly in clear lakes.

Raccoon

The number of raccoons in the state has increased dramatically. Scientists think there are more in Illinois today than there were when the first European settlers arrived.

Redheaded Woodpecker

Redheaded woodpeckers have become more scarce in Illinois, in part because their habitat is threatened. Their diet includes insects, seeds, nuts, and corn.

Economy

Abraham Lincoln Presidential Library and Museum

In addition to the Abraham Lincoln Presidential Library and Museum, tourists in Springfield can visit many other sites devoted to the 16th president, including his home, law offices, and tomb.

Tourism

A popular tourist destination, Illinois is one of the 10 most-visited states in the country. Chicago's parks, festivals, and museums are key attractions. The Field Museum displays collections from the World's Columbian Exposition of 1893 as well as mummies, meteorites, and dinosaurs. Young tourists visiting Chicago's lakefront are enthralled by Navy Pier and its exciting playground.

Illinois also boasts many important historical memories. The memory of Abraham Lincoln draws visitors to Springfield. The Abraham Lincoln Presidential Library and Museum opened in 2005, featuring state-of-the-art exhibits about the president's life and times. In Galena, visitors can see the home of President Ulysses S. Grant, as well as a feast of architecture and history blended with art galleries, shopping, and other attractions.

Chicago

Important architects designed many of Chicago's notable structures. Visitors enjoy taking tours to explore the city and its buildings.

Field Museum

Sue, a dinosaur skeleton, is one of the most popular exhibits at the Field Museum. It is one of the world's largest, most complete Tyrannosaurus Rex fossils ever discovered.

Navy Pier

Chicago's Navy Pier features a children's museum, theaters, an indoor ice-skating rink, a miniature golf course, and a 150-foot-high Ferris wheel that provides a stunning view of the city's skyline.

Hog farming generates more than $1 billion towards the Illinois economy.

Primary Industries

Illinois's history of farming has led to some important agricultural developments. Blacksmith William Parlin settled in Illinois in 1840 and began manufacturing plows soon after. He helped develop many devices, such as stalk cutters and double plows, that eased the difficult work of the farmer.

Although fewer than 4 percent of U.S. farms are in Illinois, the state is among the top agricultural producers in the nation. It ranks high in feed grains, corn, and soybeans. More than three-fourths of the land in Illinois is used for agriculture. Hogs are the most important livestock in Illinois, and the state consistently ranks near the top in U.S. hog production. The manufacturing of farm and construction machinery is vital to the state economy. Chemicals, transportation equipment, and plastic and rubber goods also are key products made in Illinois.

Illinois has approximately

74,300 farms.

Boeing, McDonald's, and **United Airlines** all call Illinois home.

Value of Goods and Services (in Millions of Dollars)

While Illinois has a significant manufacturing industry, the state makes most of its money from finance, insurance, and real estate, and from information and professional services. What sector contributes the least amount of money to the state? Why might this be the case?

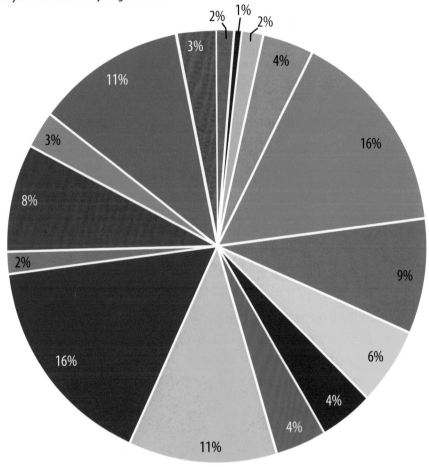

● Agriculture, Forestry, and Fishing	$10,609	● Media and Entertainment	$24,886
● Mining	$2,727	● Finance, Insurance, and Real Estate	$71,978
● Utilities	$9,922	● Professional and Technical Services	$103,709
● Construction	$25,417	● Education	$10,502
● Manufacturing	$99,665	● Health Care and Social Services	$51,497
● Wholesale Trade	$55,240	● Hotels and Restaurants	$18,588
● Retail Trade	$37,995	● Government	$18,061
● Transportation and Warehousing	$27,294	● Other Services	$73,317

Caterpillar is the leading manufacturer of construction and mining equipment. The company's headquarters are located in Peoria, Illinois.

Goods and Services

Illinois's agricultural bounty is tied to the state's importance in food processing. Many of the nation's largest food corporations are headquartered in Illinois. Food products that are made in factories across the state include sausages, dairy products, and breakfast cereals.

Technology is another key component of the Illinois economy. Computers and other electronic goods, such as wireless telephones, Internet-access products, and **embedded** electronic systems, are produced in the Chicago area. Also important is biotechnology. Several of the nation's largest manufacturers of health-care products and **pharmaceuticals** are headquartered in northern Illinois.

Since before the Civil War, iron and steel mills have always been an important industry in the Chicago area.

Doctors, lawyers, teachers, and government employees are among the part of the workforce employed in the service sector. A large portion of the service sector caters to groups and businesses that head to Chicago for the many **conventions** and trade shows that are held there each year. These meetings generate much revenue for the state and provide employment for many people in the tourism industry, such as hotel clerks and restaurant workers.

Another important part of Illinois's economy is the financial industry. The state is home to more than 2,300 commercial banks, more than 2,000 insurance companies, and many other financial service corporations. Illinois also has many warehousing and distribution facilities and has a vast transportation network, making use of its central location in the United States.

Argonne National Laboratory is a science and engineering research center. It employs roughly 3,400 people and is located in Lemont, Illinois.

Being centrally located in the country, Illinois is a major hub for transporting and warehousing goods.

The Kaskaskia Native Americans were one of the many tribes that made up the Illiniwek Confederation. They lived in the Great Lakes region.

Native Americans

The first residents of Illinois, thousands of years ago, moved with the seasons to places that had available plants and animals. A group of Native Americans established large towns there in about 700 AD. These Native Americans also built mounds of earth as temples and burial grounds.

The Mound Builders introduced corn from Mexico, invented hoes made of flint to **till** the land, and created bows and arrows for hunting. The community of Cahokia, in western Illinois, had about 20,000 people around the year 1200, making it one of the largest cities in the world at the time.

By the time the first European explorers arrived in the 1600s, Illinois was populated by the Illiniwek, a loose **confederation** of

12 independent Native American groups. The Illiniwek established a peaceful society based on agriculture and hunting. By the 1700s, seven of the Illiniwek groups had migrated or merged with the other Illinois groups. Attacks by invaders killed many of the Illiniwek. By the early 1800s, the Kaskaskia and the Peoria were the only Illiniwek groups who remained.

Black Hawk was a war leader and chief of the Sauk Native American group.

Exploring the Land

The first European explorers of the Illinois region came from France. In 1673, Louis Jolliet and a missionary, Father Jacques Marquette, traveled down the Mississippi River and then up the Illinois River. They came upon the Kaskaskia, who welcomed them.

Timeline of Settlement

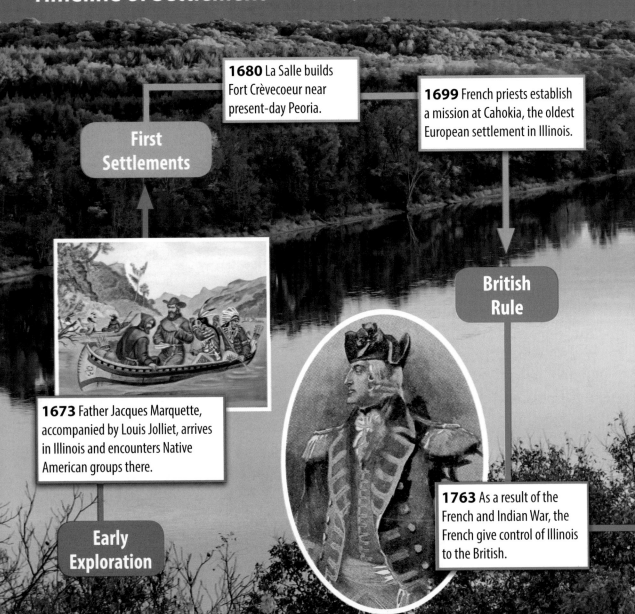

1680 La Salle builds Fort Crèvecoeur near present-day Peoria.

1699 French priests establish a mission at Cahokia, the oldest European settlement in Illinois.

First Settlements

British Rule

1673 Father Jacques Marquette, accompanied by Louis Jolliet, arrives in Illinois and encounters Native American groups there.

1763 As a result of the French and Indian War, the French give control of Illinois to the British.

Early Exploration

In 1680, the French explorer René-Robert Cavelier, sieur de La Salle, entered Illinois and established Fort Crèvecoeur along the Illinois River. Two years later, he and Henri de Tonti built Fort St. Louis atop a bluff in what is now Starved Rock State Park. The fort served as a major fur-trading post for many years. Soon, settlements began to spring up.

Marquette returned in 1675, and started the first Roman Catholic mission among the Kaskaskia. French priests soon established several other missions in Illinois. Under these missions, many of Illinois's Native Americans converted to Christianity.

Territory and Statehood

1779 Jean-Baptist-Point du Sable builds a trading post along the Chicago River, at the site of what will become Chicago.

1787 Congress passes the Northwest Ordinance, establishing the Northwest Territory, which includes Illinois.

1803 U.S. troops build Fort Dearborn on the future site of Chicago.

1778 George Rogers Clark of Virginia and his men defeat the British at Kaskaskia.

1809 The Illinois Territory is established.

American Revolutionary War

1818 Illinois becomes a state.

French settlers were some of the first Europeans in Illinois. Many of them traveled into Illinois from Canada.

The First Settlers

Stories of the friendly Native American groups and great hunting opportunities in Illinois lured many early European settlers to the area. A mission in Cahokia became the first permanent European settlement in the state. In 1703, French missionaries established the town of Kaskaskia, named after one of the local American Indian groups.

Fur trading flourished as more immigrants arrived, attracted by the massive herds of bison roaming the area. More forts and settlements were soon established. The arrival of the French fur traders changed the Native Americans' traditional economy and caused them to be dependent on the French.

The British saw the fur-trading value of the Illinois region and soon challenged the French for control, in the French and American Indian War. Native American groups took sides with either the French or the British. The British defeated the French in 1763. Many French settlers and Native Americans, unhappy with the transfer of power, left Illinois.

After the American Revolutionary War, settlement in Illinois increased. Most settlers chose to build their homes in the south. The first settlement in northern Illinois, built around Fort Dearborn, developed into the city of Chicago. Treaties with the Native Americans made more land available to settlers. Many Native Americans were not content with the terms of the treaties, however. When war broke out between the United States and Great Britain in 1812, many Native American groups supported Great Britain in the hopes that they would have their land returned.

The United States won the war, and increasing numbers of settlers began to arrive from the East. Between 1818 and 1830, the population of Illinois more than quadrupled. Kaskaskia became the state's first capital in 1809, and Vandalia its second in 1819. In 1839, the capital was moved from Vandalia to Springfield under pressure from Abraham Lincoln, and by 1848, almost one million people lived in Illinois.

Fort Dearborn was built along the Chicago River. It eventually grew into the city of Chicago.

History Makers

Many notable Illinoisans contributed to development of their state and country. President Ronald Reagan was born in Illinois, and three other presidents lived in the state before becoming president. They were Abraham Lincoln, Ulysses S. Grant, and Barack Obama. In addition, a number of social reformers have come from the Prairie State. In recent times, Hillary Rodham Clinton, who was born in Chicago and grew up in Park Ridge, served as the First Lady of the United States when her husband, Bill Clinton, was president. She became secretary of state in 2009.

Abraham Lincoln (1809–1865)

Abraham Lincoln settled in Illinois when he was 21. He studied law and served in the state legislature. During an unsuccessful bid for a U.S. Senate seat in 1858, he engaged in a series of debates with Stephen Douglas. Lincoln argued that slavery should not be allowed in new states. Lincoln was elected president in 1860, and the Civil War began the next year. The new president faced the difficult task of keeping the Union together, guiding the nation through the war, and attempting to end slavery. He was **assassinated** in April 1865.

Jane Addams (1860–1935)

Jane Addams was born in Cedarville. While traveling in Europe, she visited a **settlement house** and decided to open a similar institution for the poor in Chicago. Hull House, which opened in 1889, was one of the first settlement houses in the U.S., providing aid, food, and education for thousands of people.

Ronald Reagan (1911–2004)

Ronald Reagan was born in Tampico and grew up in Dixon. He moved to California in 1937 to become an actor. Reagan appeared in a number of movies and became involved in politics after serving as president of a major actors' **union**. He was elected governor of California in 1966. In 1980, he was elected president of the United States. During his two terms in office, he cut taxes, increased military spending, and improved relations with the Soviet Union.

Harold Washington (1922–1987)

Harold Washington was born in Chicago. He grew up there, graduated from Roosevelt University, and received a law degree from Northwestern University. Washington served in the Illinois state legislature and then in the U.S. House of Representatives. In 1983, he was elected as the first African American mayor of Chicago. He worked to reform Chicago's government and politics.

Barack Obama (1961–)

Barack Obama was born in Honolulu, Hawai'i. After graduating from law school in 1991, he worked in Chicago. In 1996, he was elected to the Illinois Senate. Eight years later, he was elected to the U.S. Senate. In 2009, he became the 44th U.S. president, the first African American to hold the position.

Culture

More than 44,000 students are enrolled at the University of Illinois, Urbana-Champaign.

More than 400,000 people commute into Chicago from the surrounding suburbs in order to work every day.

The People Today

More than 12.8 million people live in Illinois, making it one of the most populous states in the country. Most Illinoisans live in cities and towns. Fewer than 15 percent live in rural areas. With the exception of Springfield, which lies near the center of the state, most of the state's largest cities are located in northern Illinois.

Chicago has a population of more than 2.8 million residents. Including surrounding suburbs and smaller cities, the population of the Chicago metropolitan area soars to 9.8 million. Many of the state's largest cities, such as Aurora, Naperville, Elgin, and Cicero, are part of the Chicago metropolitan area.

Although the vast majority of Illinoisans were born in the United States, the state's immigrant population began to increase greatly in the 1990s. Today, almost 17 percent of the population is Hispanic or Latino, only slightly less than the national average. About 15 percent of Illinois's people are African American. Native Americans, though once numerous in the region, now make up less than 1 percent of Illinois's population. People of German, British, Irish, Polish, and Italian ancestry have a long history as residents of Illinois.

The population of Illinois has **grown** steadily in the past **60 years**.

Q What are the different factors that contribute to a state's population growth?

The current state capitol of Illinois is the 6th building to be used for this purpose.

State Government

The state adopted its first constitution in 1818. New constitutions were adopted in 1848, 1870, and 1970. Illinois's government, like the federal government, is made up of three branches. They are the executive, the legislative, and the judicial branches.

The executive branch is headed by the governor. The governor appoints officials, sets budgets, and has the authority to **veto** bills passed by the legislature. A new governor is elected every four years.

The legislative branch is the state legislature, which is called the General Assembly. It is made up of the Senate, with 59 members, and the House of Representatives, with 118 members. The legislative branch passes new laws and changes existing ones.

The judicial branch consists of the state's courts. The state's highest court is the Illinois Supreme Court. It has seven justices who are elected to 10-year terms.

In 2011, the Illinois capitol building underwent a $50 million renovation. Facilities were upgraded, but work was also done to bring the building back to its 1870s appearance.

Bruce Rauner is the 42nd governor of Illinois. He was sworn in on January 12, 2015.

Illinois's state song is called
"Illinois."

*By thy rivers gently flowing,
Illinois, Illinois,
O'er thy prairies verdant growing,
Illinois, Illinois,
Comes an echo on the breeze.
Rustling through the leafy trees, and its
mellow tones are these,
Illinois, Illinois,
And its mellow tones are these, Illinois.
From a wilderness of prairies,
Illinois, Illinois,
Straight thy way and never varies,
Illinois, Illinois,
Till upon the inland sea, Stands thy
great commercial tree, turning all the
world to thee, Illinois, Illinois,*

Turning all the world to thee, Illinois.

* excerpted

The Puerto Rican Festival in Chicago features a parade, live music, and food vendors.

Celebrating Culture

With so many different ethnic groups and heritages, Illinois has a rich mix of cultures. People from nearly every country in the world live in Illinois. Chicago is one of the most ethnically diverse cities in the United States.

Illinois has a large Hispanic-American population. To celebrate their culture, many Mexican Americans take part in the Fiesta del Sol in Chicago. It is one of the largest Mexican festivals in the nation.

During the first half of the 1900s, many African Americans left the Southern states in search of greater freedom and work in the North. By 1918, some 60,000 African Americans called Chicago home. By 1950, that number had risen to nearly 500,000, and by 1970, it had surpassed 1 million.

African American culture blossomed in Chicago in the early to mid-1900s, especially the jazz and blues music scene. Many New Orleans musicians, including jazz great Louis Armstrong, came to Chicago. This started the Chicago style of jazz. The Chicago style of blues emerged with musicians such as Muddy Waters and Howlin' Wolf. They added electric instruments to the acoustic Southern blues style and gave their music a loud beat.

Louis Armstrong made his first recordings in Chicago, Illinois, in 1922.

Illinoisans from other backgrounds celebrate their heritage in a variety of ways. Jordbruksdagarna, or Agricultural Days, is a traditional Swedish harvest festival held every September in Bishop Hill, a community in west-central Illinois. People can experience traditional Swedish music, games, and food. The Irish community paints Chicago green during the annual St. Patrick's Day festivities. The Polish community keeps its culture alive through traditional dances and museums that showcase its history and culture.

The St. Patrick's Day parade and celebration in Chicago always happens on the Saturday on or before St. Patrick's Day. The Chicago River is famously dyed green for the day.

Ernest Hemingway was born in Oak Park, Illinois. He is best known for his novels, *The Old Man and The Sea* and *A Farewell to Arms*.

Arts and Entertainment

Illinois is a hub of arts and entertainment. Many talented children's writers have come from the state. For example, Shel Silverstein, a Chicago native, wrote and illustrated many books, including *A Light in the Attic* and *The Giving Tree*. Ernest Hemingway is one of the state's most notable authors. In 1954, he won the Nobel Prize for Literature. His novels and short stories earned him a reputation as one of the greatest writers of the twentieth century.

Music is a strong part of Illinois's culture. Several opera groups have entertained audiences since the early 1900s, and choirs and orchestras showcase talented musicians and singers. Jazz, blues, and folk music have also developed in the state. Blues musicians flocked to Chicago in the early 1920s, and the city has been a blues capital ever since.

Gwendolyn Brooks, raised in Chicago, was the first **African American woman** to win a **Pulitzer prize** for poetry.

The **Ferris wheel**, a favorite in carnivals all across the world, was invented in **Illinois** in 1893 by **George Ferris**.

Numerous talented actors, comedians, and television personalities are from Illinois. Comedian and actor Robin Williams was born in Chicago. He became popular for his energetic style of comedy as well as his dramatic acting abilities. Hollywood star Harrison Ford was born in Chicago and raised in Park Ridge. His roles in the *Star Wars* movies and the *Indiana Jones* series ignited his acting career.

Robin Williams's most famous role as a voice actor was as the Genie in Disney's *Aladdin*.

Jane Lynch, the star of the TV show *Glee* and many movies, was born and raised in Dolton. Betty White, who has been a popular entertainer for many years, was born in Oak Park. Keke Palmer, of the Nickelodeon series *True Jackson, VP,* hails from Harvey. Oprah Winfrey was born in Mississippi, but she has lived and worked in Chicago for most of her adult life. *The Oprah Winfrey Show*, which made Winfrey one of the most popular women in the nation, ended its run in 2011, after 25 years.

The Chicago Blues Festival is the largest free blues festival in the world.

Sports and Recreation

It is easy to stay active in Illinois. Throughout the state, there are many lakes and rivers that are ideal for swimming, fishing, and boating. Illinoisans can also bike and hike in the hills and valleys of the state's many parks.

There is no shortage of professional sports in Illinois. The Chicago Bulls dominated the National Basketball Association (NBA) during the 1990s, winning six championships. In 1998, the Bulls lost many of their big-name stars, including Michael Jordan. Still, loyal fans continue to cheer for the team.

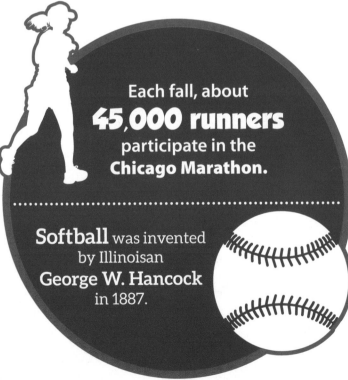

Each fall, about **45,000 runners** participate in the **Chicago Marathon.**

Softball was invented by Illinoisan **George W. Hancock** in 1887.

The Chicago Bulls were established in 1966.

Chicago has two major league baseball teams. The Chicago Cubs, who pack fans into Wrigley Field, won the World Series in 1907 and 1908. The Chicago White Sox, who play in U.S. Cellular Field, won the World Series in 1906, 1917, and 2005. Illinois also was the birthplace of women's baseball. During World War II, Philip Wrigley, owner of the Chicago Cubs and the Wrigley chewing gum company, started the All-American Girls Professional Baseball League.

Football fans look to the Chicago Bears for exciting action. The Bears won the Super Bowl in 1986. In 1997, the Bears became the first team in National Football League history to win 600 games.

Chicago athletes also take to the ice. The Chicago Blackhawks joined the National Hockey League in 1926. Over the years, Blackhawk heroes such as Phil Esposito and Bobby Hull made hockey an important Chicago pastime. The Blackhawks won the Stanley Cup in 1934, 1936, 1961, and 2010.

The Bears football team was founded in 1919 and has been in Chicago since 1921.

Get To Know
ILLINOIS

The **Chicago Public library** has more than **5.4 million books.**

There are about
700 airports
located throughout the state.

With **110 stories**, **Willis Tower** is one of the world's tallest buildings.

CHICAGO IS HOME TO THE **FIRST** INLAND AQUARIUM WITH A **PERMANENT** SALTWATER FISH COLLECTION IN THE U.S. THE AQUARIUM OPENED IN 1893.

The Lincoln Park Zoo, established in 1868, is one of the **oldest zoos** in the U.S.

Collinsville is home to the **world's largest catsup bottle,** standing at **170 feet.**

Illinois was the **first state** to ratify the 13th amendment to abolish slavery.

Brain Teasers

What have you learned about Illinois after reading this book? Test your knowledge by answering these questions. All of the information can be found in the text you just read. The answers are provided below for easy reference.

1 What supplies 90 percent of the state's power?

2 What Native American Confederacy populated Illinois when the first Europeans arrived?

3 What is the number one livestock animals produced in Illinois?

4 In what city is the Abraham Lincoln Presidential Library and Museum located?

5 What are the four major landforms of Illinois?

6 Approximately how many rivers and streams are in Illinois?

7 Woodlands and forests cover how many square miles of Illinois?

8 Which French explorer established Fort St. Louis?

ANSWER KEY
1. Nuclear power and coal-fired plants 2. Illiniwek 3. Hogs 4. Springfield 5. The Central Lowland, the Ozark Plateaus, the Interior Low Plateaus, and the Coastal Plain 6. 900 7. 6,400 miles 8. René-Robert Cavelier

Key Words

assassinated: murdered, often for political reasons

confederation: an alliance between groups for mutual assistance and protection

conventions: large meetings to discuss common issues and share knowledge

embedded: enclosed

glaciers: large masses of slow-moving ice

immigrants: people who move to a new country

pharmaceuticals: medicinal drugs

reserves: supplies

settlement house: a building in a poor community where services are provided for people

species: a group of animals or plants that share the same characteristics and can mate

till: to work the land in order to raise crops

union: a group of workers organized to deal collectively with employers

veto: the right to reject or block the passing of a bill or law

Index

Addams, Jane 33
African Americans 33, 35, 38, 39, 40

Chicago 5, 6, 7, 21, 24, 25, 29, 31, 32, 33, 35, 38, 39, 40, 41, 42, 43, 44, 45
Chicago River 7, 29, 31, 39
coal 14, 46

Galena 14, 21

Jolliet, Louis 28

Kaskaskia 26, 27, 28, 29, 30, 31

La Salle, René-Robert Cavelier, sieur de 28, 29
Lincoln, Abraham 20, 21, 31, 32, 46

Marquette, Father Jacques 28, 29
mounds 27
music 4, 5, 38, 39, 40

Native Americans 8, 9, 26, 27, 28, 29, 30, 31, 35, 46

Obama, Barack 32, 33

Peoria 8, 24, 27, 28

Reagan, Ronald 32, 33

Sable, Jean-Baptist-Point du 29
Shawnee Hills 10, 11
Springfield 4, 8, 20, 21, 31, 35, 46

Tonti, Henri de 29

Vandalia 31

Washington, Harold 33
Wrigley Field 43

Log on to www.av2books.com

AV² by Weigl brings you media enhanced books that support active learning. Go to www.av2books.com, and enter the special code found on page 2 of this book. You will gain access to enriched and enhanced content that supplements and complements this book. Content includes video, audio, weblinks, quizzes, a slide show, and activities.

AV² Online Navigation

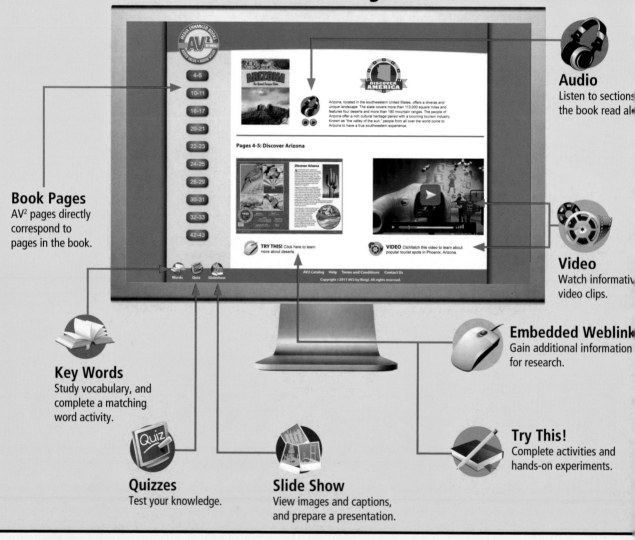

Audio
Listen to sections the book read al

Book Pages
AV² pages directly correspond to pages in the book.

Key Words
Study vocabulary, and complete a matching word activity.

Quizzes
Test your knowledge.

Slide Show
View images and captions, and prepare a presentation.

Video
Watch informativ video clips.

Embedded Weblink
Gain additional information for research.

Try This!
Complete activities and hands-on experiments.

AV² was built to bridge the gap between print and digital. We encourage you to tell us what you like and what you want to see in the future.

Sign up to be an AV² Ambassador at www.av2books.com/ambassador.

Due to the dynamic nature of the Internet, some of the URLs and activities provided as part of AV² by Weigl may have changed or ceased to exist. AV² by Weigl accepts no responsibility for any such changes. All media enhanced books are regularly monitored to update addresses and sites in a timely manner. Contact AV² by Weigl at 1-866-649-3445 or av2books@weigl.com with any questions, comments, or feedback.

CARMEL CLAY PUBLIC LIBRARY
Renewal Line: (317) 814-3936
www.carmel.lib.in.us

Withdrawn from
Carmel Clay Public Library